CONTENTS

KU-580-941

SIMPLY
KARATE

HINKLER
BOOKS

Author: Mark Richardson
Art Director: Karen Moores
Photography: Glenn Weiss
Graphic Artist: Susie Allen
Special thanks to: Katie Richardson

Published in 2005
by Hinkler Books Pty Ltd
17-23 Redwood Drive
Dingley, VIC 3172, Australia
www.hinklerbooks.com

© Hinkler Books Pty Ltd 2005

Printed and bound in China

ISBN 1 7412 1601 X

INTRODUCTION

Hello and welcome to SIMPLY KARATE. Throughout history, many people have enjoyed the individual benefits of studying karate. Now your opportunity to practise conscientiously at home has arrived.

The following is either the beginning of an exciting new journey as a karate-ka (karate student or follower), or a useful reference guide and training tool for the karate-ka who has already begun karate-do (the study of karate).

This book is a guide to the basic karate etiquette, attitude, technique and application explained to you on the DVD, and includes an explanatory syllabus of techniques and terminology. These are the foundation of your karate and should be rehearsed by the beginner and the advanced student alike.

Please use this book and the accompanying DVD for inspiration, motivation, and as an instruction manual to aid your karate technique.

Best wishes and enjoy SIMPLY KARATE.

Mark

KARATE HISTORY

Karate literally translated is 'kara' (empty), and 'te' (hand), or *way of the empty hand*. In the modern world, the form of martial art we know as 'karate' was born in Japan. Some pundits would argue that it is common knowledge that karate originated in Okinawa. However, this martial art has an extensive history, so to simplify and to save argument, the majority would agree that 'karate' is Japanese and 'Okinawa-te' has most of its history in Okinawa.

As modern karate has its differing styles, with their emphasis and influences that make them their own, so does Okinawa-te with its development in several regions of the country. To unravel the history of Okinawa-te, one would have to search the surrounding countries (even Japan itself) and their fighting systems for answers of its true origins. There are differing opinions, so perhaps you may search for the history of the art yourself and make up your own mind.

What is clear however, is that historically weapons were outlawed in Okinawa, hence the need for the study of unarmed self-defence. For this reason Okinawa-te was generally studied in small groups or passed on to a single student. Although the development of Okinawa-te was extensive, it was not until the art was accepted in Japan that its growing popularity soon had people studying karate in the masses.

Now karate, with its colourful and traditional background and strong elements of modern competition, can be found in most countries of the world through the masters and their students of the individual styles.

As you can see, karate has developed over a very long period of time. Hopefully your love for the art may influence the evolution of karate in coming generations.

THE BENEFITS OF KARATE

STRENGTH OF BODY

Karate will ultimately affect your whole body. Your flexibility will increase, along with your physical fitness, and as a consequence your strength and stamina will also improve. If you fall in love with the art of karate as I have, you will develop a devotion to the fitness aspect of your training as you concentrate more and more on perfecting your technique, speed and power. Your karate and your body will both benefit.

STRENGTH OF MIND

Karate will give you the ability to focus your mind. As a technical art, training for karate involves setting goals. For example, a realistic long-term goal could be to be able to complete the DVD class from start to finish with good posture, stance, technique and speed, keeping up with the class. As you focus on short-term goals, for example concentrating on good stance, you will find that each successful step will draw you closer to the big goal. The same formula can be applied with meditation and prayer to everything you do in life. Continuous practice will give you a strong mind.

SPEED OF RESPONSE AND AWARENESS

The physical study of karate requires a reflex response. Improvement of the speed of this response requires mental awareness of your own body and your surrounding environment. Increased awareness and speed of your response is achieved through repetition.

STRENGTH OF CHARACTER

As your body adapts to Karate training and your mind becomes focused and more alert, you will find yourself achieving your goals with your karate. Your confidence will grow, and application to other aspects of your life will have similar results. An attitude of humility will equally accompany your confidence, always remembering where you began. Karate masters and teachers who have been training for the better part of their lives are still training hard, ever improving and striving for perfection. The realisation of this fact will spur you on to do the same, with strong character.

Karate helps you develop the strength of your body, and of your mind. Your speed of response and awareness will also increase with study. Karate ultimately strengthens your character.

Osu!

KARATE FOCUS

ENJOY THE INCREMENTAL PROCESS

Anyone can study the art of karate. However, karate is a physically demanding art, so it is advisable to begin slowly. I can understand your enthusiasm, which is fantastic, but be aware of your body's limitations. By all means, set goals to execute your techniques faster, higher, and with more stamina, but do not hurt yourself by doing so. One of the greatest attributes of the human body is that it will adapt to just about anything we physically demand of it. Therefore, the smallest increases that you demand of your body will have a positive effect. Make your short-term goals small and incremental. This will ensure that you become increasingly confident every time you step into your dojo.

HAVE A STRONG 'KIAI'

As your karate progresses, begin to focus less on the TV, placing it more in your peripheral vision. Picture an imaginary person in front of you. Make a point of learning exactly where every strike, punch and so on lands on your opponent's body. When you are training in the DVD class, 'Kiai' (yell) strongly at the end (focus point) of every technique. This emphasis on the focus point will help ensure that your technique is strong – i.e. your posture and stance, legs, trunk and torso, along with your strike. Your 'Kiai' (ki – meaning energy) will focus your mind and body on the exact technique you wish to achieve. Your 'Kiai' needs to be LOUD, so exhale all your breath as you yell. This will tense and strengthen your mid-section and make you feel that every part of your body has gone into your technique. I advise, for the sake of ease, to yell the actual word 'Kiai', pronounced ki-ai.

TAKE THE TIME TO MEDITATE

The purpose of meditation is to focus – firstly, that the following class will provide improvement, and secondly, to reflect upon your completed training session. Be aware of your strengths and memorise areas that may need more attention. Meditation and prayer promote positive self-improvement in your karate as well as in other areas of your life. There is no time during meditation for negative reflection. This exercise alone will greatly improve your karate as it allows you to examine your own training objectively, giving your study direction and purpose.

THE BOW-IN
THE BEGINNING OF THE CLASS

Entering the Dojo

At the entrance of the dojo (place of training) it is customary to remove your shoes and bow before stepping on to the dojo floor. The bow is accompanied with a strong 'Osu' (pronounced 'Oss'). 'Osu' is a word given to an attitude ever-present in the dojo, a temperament best described as humility, respect, discernment, courtesy and perseverance. (Although the best description is learned through experience.) Continually developed over time from the moment you begin karate, it is the student's goal to refine this attitude so that it becomes a way of life in and out of the training hall. The dojo is highly respected, as it is a place where people come to develop their inner character and physical body through the art of karate, hence the acknowledgment when entering.

'Ready' stance - pre

STAND IN 'READY' STANCE - YOI DACHI

1 Upright posture

2 Shoulders relaxed

3 Arms crossed with fists at opposite shoulders

4 Feet shoulder-width apart and pigeon-toed 45 degrees inward

5 Block down with both arms as your feet move 45 degrees outward

6 Fists positioned approx. two fist-lengths in front of each thigh

7 Elbows and knees slightly bent

'Ready' stance - final

MOVE IN TO 'FORMAL ATTENTION' STANCE - MUSUBI DACHI

1 Upright posture

2 Shoulders relaxed

3 Both hands in knife hand position (fingers together, thumbs pulled down), one hand overlaps the other, palms toward your face, fingertips pointed to the ceiling and just under eye level, elbows pointed down

4 As the hands come together your feet come together also, heels touching, feet 45 degrees outward, knees slightly bent

5 Hands fold down in to dove-tail position, hands overlapping and approx. two fist-lengths in front of the body, thumbs interlocked

'Formal Attention' stance - pre

'Formal Attention' stance - final

Move into a Kneeling Position - Seiza

1 Kneel the left knee on the floor followed by the right knee
2 Position both fists on their respective thighs, just below the hip bone.
3 Knees approx. two fist-lengths apart and left big toe placed lightly on the right
4 Upright posture
5 Shoulders relaxed

Close your Eyes - Mokuso

1 Concentrate on your breathing
2 Clear your mind
3 Meditate on the training session to come. Open your eyes 'Mokuso Yame'

Bow to the Front - Shinzen Ni Rei

1 Bow to God and to the acknowledgment and respect of the karate masters
2 Both fists go to the floor approx. two fist-lengths in front of the knees
3 Bowing forward, the elbows bend as your head nearly touches the floor
4 Move straight back to kneeling position 'Seiza'

Bow to the Front Again - Sosai Ni Rei

1 Bow to the front, this time in acknowledgment and respect of the master and founder of the particular style of karate you study
2 Both fists go to the floor approx. two fist-lengths in front of the knees
3 Bowing forward, the elbows bend as your head nearly touches the floor
4 As you bow say 'Osu!'
5 Move straight back to kneeling position 'Seiza'. Stand up and move into 'Ready' stance 'Yoi Dachi'. Now you are ready to begin the warm-up!

THE BODY WARM-UP

Purpose *The purpose of these exercises is to 'warm up' the body. Warming the muscles and joints prior to both your stretching and the main training session will greatly reduce the risk of injury. Depending on your physical strength or fitness level you may want to modify your exercises or increase/decrease the number of repetitions so that the 'warm-up' is just that – a warm-up. This section should not leave you absolutely drained so that you can't continue the next part of the class, but also should raise the temperature of the body sufficiently to proceed with stretches without injury.*

STAR JUMPS

1 Arms come up 45 degrees or higher to the side
2 At the same time, the legs jump out creating an 'X' or star
3 Aim for 60 repetitions

RUNNING ON THE SPOT

1 Jog lightly on the spot for 5 seconds
2 Sprint on the spot for 5 seconds
3 Aim for 6 of each

HOP DROPS

1 Drop down into a squat

2 Come back up with a small jump

3 Aim for 30 repetitions

PUSH-UPS ON THE KNUCKLES

1 Fists on the floor directly below the shoulders

2 Raise your body off the floor drawing your stomach in to your spine

3 Shoulders, hips, knees and ankles should be in line with each other

4 Bend the elbows at right angles so your chest and chin are nearly to the floor

5 Elbows stay close to the ribs as you execute your push-ups

6 Aim for 10 repetitions

7 Try modifications on your knees, on your hands, or both

As your strength and fitness increases, also increase the length of time and the amount of repetitions used, so you're sufficiently warmed up for the stretching.

JOINT WARM-UP & MUSCLE STRETCH

Purpose *The purpose of warming up the joints and stretching the muscles is to maximise your flexibility and provide the greatest range of movement for your body. Your goal is to stretch your body to the range of movement that it is most capable of. However, aiming to stretch the body further than it was previously capable of should be reserved until after the training session when the body is very warm, so as not to decrease or impede the performance of your karate technique.*

1 Hands on your belt or hips. Begin with the first side

2 Stretch the toes – big toe up whilst the others stretch down, then opposite, 10 times

3 Raise the knee and rotate the knee and ankle both ways, 10 times

4 Point the toes and extend the ankle into 'instep' or top of foot position 'Heisoku', hold for 5 seconds

5 Keep the ankle extended pointing the foot, and pull the toes back into 'ball of the foot' position 'Chusoku', hold for 5 seconds

6 Pull the foot back pushing the heel forward into the 'heel' position 'Kakato', hold for 5 seconds

7 Heel to the floor, reaching your hands to your toes, stretching the hamstring, hold for 10 seconds

8 Extend the leg to the side with the 'knife edge of the foot' position, big toe up and other toes down, foot horizontal 'Sokuto' hold for 5 seconds

9 Raise the knee 'Hiza' as high as you can, stretching the hip flexors, hold for 10 seconds

10 Bend the knee and hold the foot from behind 'Ushiro' with both hands, stretching the quadriceps, hold for 10 seconds

11 Hold your ankle, raising your shin horizontally to the side 'Yoko', stretching your adductors and your hamstrings, hold for 10 seconds

Shake and loosen your working leg. Repeat all of these steps with the other leg.

12 Rock on to the toes and the heels forward and back, stretching and flexing the calf and achilles 10 times

13 Tilt the head forward and back, stretching and loosening the neck 10 times

14 Turn the head side to side, stretching and loosening the neck 10 times

15 Neck – tilt the head, shoulder to shoulder, stretching and loosening the neck 10 times

16 Rotate the shoulders forward and reverse 10 times

17 Horizontally flex and extend the arms, stretching the chest and back 10 times

18 Rotate the arms forward and reverse, loosening the shoulders 10 times

19 Rotate the elbows and wrists inward and outward 10 times

20 Raise arms and turn the spine right and left 10 times

21 Laterally stretch the spine right and left, hold for 10 seconds each

22 Hang forward stretch the spine, flexing at the hips and trunk, hold for 10 seconds

23 Lean back stretching the spine, hyper-extending the back, stretching the abdominal area, hold for 10 seconds

JOINT WARM-UP & MUSCLE STRETCH

(continued)

24 Rotate the hips right and left 10 times

25 Rotate the knees and ankles right and left 10 times

26 Squat then straighten the legs, stretching the hamstrings 3 times

27 Legs – firstly, feet double shoulder-width apart, forearms on the knees pushing outward, stretch the groin, then straighten the legs and stretch the hamstrings, hold for 10 seconds. Secondly, feet double shoulder-width apart, place the hands to front, then the middle, then behind, stretching the hamstrings, hold each for 10 seconds

28 Legs – feet double shoulder width apart, both hands toward the right foot, keep the knee straight, stretch the hamstrings (repeat with other leg) hold for 10 seconds

29 Legs – 3 count leg stretch exercise, hold each for 10 seconds

1 Right adductor (inner thigh) stretch – face the front, lean left, bending the left knee, keeping the leg straight and the right foot horizontal

2 Hip flexor, calf and achilles stretch – turn and face left, lean forward, left knee bent and right leg straight

3 Right hamstring and glute stretch – turn and face right and lean left, left knee bent and right leg straight
(repeat all three counts for the left leg)

30 Front splits – adductors (inner thigh) stretch, facing the front, legs straight out to the side, feet flat on the floor, hold for 10 seconds

31 Front splits – hamstring and adductors (inner thigh) stretch, facing the front, legs straight out to the side, heels on the floor, toes pointed upward, hold for 10 seconds

32 Left side splits – left hamstring and right adductors (inner thigh), turn and face left, left leg straight with toes upward, right leg straight with foot horizontal in 'Sokuto' flat on the floor, hold for 10 seconds

33 Left side splits – left hamstring and right hip flexor, turn and face left, left leg straight with toes upward, right leg straight with knee and instep of foot facing the floor, hold for 10 seconds (Repeat step 32 & 33 on the right side. Then sit, facing the front, keeping the legs apart)

34 Right hamstring and left lats – right hand to the right foot, and left hand over the head to the right foot, hold for 10 seconds (Repeat to the left)

35 Double hamstring and groin stretch – left hand to the left foot, right hand to the right foot, chest to the floor, hold for 10 seconds

36 Double hamstring and calf stretch – legs to the front, knees straight, hold the ball of the foot and pull the feet back, chest to the knees, hold for 10 seconds

37 Groin and glute stretch – heels in, hold the feet, pull the chest to the feet, hold for 10 seconds

38 Groin stretch – hold the ankles, elbow on the knees, pushing the knees to the floor, hold for 10 seconds

39 Double quad stretch – kneeling 'Seiza', lean back onto your hands, elbows, or shoulders, hold for 10 seconds.

Stand up in 'Ready' stance 'Yoi Dachi'

PUNCHES

These particular karate punches strike varying parts of the body and are used holding a fist 'Seiken'. Close the fingers into the palm of your hand, then bend and wrap the thumb over the first two fingers, squeeze the fist tight with your little finger. Shout with a loud 'Kiai' whilst executing your punches.

Practise these punches with the right foot forward in the 'Hour Glass' stance 'Migi Sanchin Dachi'. Be aware of the relationship between a good stance and the power developed through the foot and respective punching arm.

HOUR GLASS STANCE - MIGI SANCHIN

1 From 'Yoi Dachi' draw your right arm in, crossing at the forearms

2 At the same time draw the right foot in towards the left, centring your weight

3 Move your feet into the hour glass stance as you double-block up and out with a 'Kiai'

4 Keep your posture straight

5 Bend at the knees

MID-SECTION PUNCH - CHUDAN TSUKI

1 Prepare by placing the left fist, centred at solar plexus height

2 Position the right fist palm up at the ribs

3 Turn the hips and execute the right-side punch first

4 Turn the wrist at the last second and 'Kiai'

5 Keep a good stance and posture and repeat 30 times

UPPER PUNCH - JODAN TSUKI

1 Prepare by placing the left fist, centred at chin height

2 Position the right fist palm up at the ribs

3 Turn the hips and execute the right-side punch first

4 Turn the wrist at the last second as you 'Kiai'

5 Keep a good stance and posture and repeat 30 times

PUNCHES

(continued)

LOWER PUNCH - GEDAN TSUKI

1 Prepare by placing the left fist, centred to the groin or top of the pubic bone

2 Position the right fist palm up at the ribs

3 Turn the hips and execute the right-side punch first

4 Turn the wrist at the last second and 'Kiai'

5 Keep a good stance and posture and repeat 30 times

JAB TO THE CHIN - AGO UCHI

1 Place both arms shoulder-width apart by your sides, fists at shoulder height

2 Turn the hips and execute the right-side punch first

3 Pull the punch straight back to the original position with speed

4 Turn the wrist at the last second and 'Kiai'

5 Keep a good stance and posture and repeat 30 times

ROUND HOOK PUNCH TO THE HEAD - MAWASHI UCHI

1 Place the left fist, through the centre at temple height, palm forward, elbow bent

2 Position the right fist palm up at the ribs

3 Draw the left forearm back for head cover, and the right arm behind your back

4 Turn the hips and execute the right-side punch first with a 'Kiai'

5 Keep a good stance and posture and repeat 30 times

BLOCKS

Be patient when learning the blocks and refer to the DVD often, as they take some coordination at first. These blocks are important, as they are the foundation of your defensive technique. Execute your blocks with your hands in a fist 'Seiken', using a loud 'Kiai'.

Practise these blocks with the left foot forward in the 'Hour Glass' stance 'Hidari Sanchin Dachi'. Be aware of the relationship between a good stance and the power developed through the foot and respective punching arm.

1 From 'Yoi Dachi' draw your left arm in, crossing at the forearms

2 At the same time draw the left foot in towards the right, centring your weight

3 Move the same foot left into the 'Hour Glass' stance as you double-block with a 'Kiai'

4 Keep your posture straight

5 Bend the knees slightly

MID-SECTION BLOCK - CHUDAN SOTO UKE

1 Left arm in block position, right fist pulled back at ribs under armpit

2 Right fist behind the right ear, elbow back, left fist at the opposite ribs under armpit

3 Turn the hips and block across to the left with the right arm at the mid-section

4 Turn the wrist at the last second, blocking a strike or kick to the solar plexus

5 Keep your posture straight, bend at the knees, repeat 30 times

MID-SECTION BLOCK - CHUDAN UCHI UKE

1 Right fist at the opposite ribs under the armpit

2 Left fist pointed to the opponent

3 Turn the hips and execute the right-side block across to the right at the mid-section

4 Turn the wrist at the last second, blocking a strike or kick to the solar plexus

5 Keep your posture straight, bending at the knees, repeat 30 times

BLOCKS

(continued)

UPPER BLOCK - JODAN UKE

1 Left arm diagonally above the head

2 Right fist by the right ribs under the armpit

3 Turn the hips, right arm up in front of the face, blocking diagonally

4 Turn the wrist at the last second, blocking a strike to the head with a 'Kiai'

5 Keep your posture straight, bending at the knees, repeat 30 times

LOWER BLOCK - GEDAN BAR

1 Left arm in block position just in front of the left knee, right hand at the right ribs

2 Right fist palm toward the opposite ear, as the left fist covers the groin

3 Turn the hips, right arm block down to the right with a 'Kiai'

4 Turn the wrist at the last second, blocking a strike to the solar plexus or groin

5 Keep your posture straight, bending at the knees, repeat 30 times

SIMULTANEOUS MID-SECTION BLOCK AND LOWER BLOCK - CHUDAN UCHI UKE, GEDAN BARAI

1 Right hand in 'Chudan Uchi Uke' block

2 Left hand down in 'Gedan Barai' block

3 Turn the hips, draw the elbows together

4 Block down with the right arm and up to the left with the left arm with a 'Kiai'

5 Turn the wrists at the last second, blocking simultaneously, repeat 30 times

BACKFIST STRIKES

Backfist strikes use a whipping action of the fist 'Seiken', at the wrist, and have to be executed with speed. 'Kiai' loudly as you strike.

Practise these backfist strikes with the right foot forward in the 'Hour Glass' stance 'Migi Sanchin Dachi'. Be aware of the relationship between a good stance and the power developed through the foot and respective punching arm.

1 From 'Yoi Dachi' draw your right arm in, crossing at the forearms

2 At the same time draw the right foot in towards the left, centring your weight

3 Move the same foot right into the 'Hour Glass' stance as you double block with a 'Kiai'

4 Keep your posture straight

BACKFIST STRIKE TO THE FACE - URAKEN GANMEN UCHI

1 Both fists palms backward, forearms vertically together

2 Turn the hips and execute the right-side strike to the face with a 'Kiai'

3 Whip the fist at the wrist and keep the fist strong at the last second

4 Pull the arm back to the original position with speed

5 Keep a good stance and posture and repeat 30 times

BACKFIST STRIKE TO THE FACE TO THE SIDE – URAKEN SAYU UCHI

1 Both arms horizontal at sternum height, palms down, knuckles nearly touching

2 Turn the hips and execute the right-side strike to the face with a 'Kiai'

3 Whip the fist at the wrist and keep the fist strong at the last second

4 Pull the arm back to the original position with speed

5 Keep a good stance and posture and repeat 30 times

BACKFIST STRIKE TO THE SPLEEN (OR MID-SECTION) – URAKEN HIZO UCHI

1 Right fist stacked, nearly touching the left, at hip height

2 Forearms horizontal, turn the hips and execute the right-side strike to the mid-section

3 Whip the fist at the wrist and keep the fist strong at the last second with a strong 'Kiai'

4 Pull the arm back to the original position with speed

5 Keep a good stance and posture and repeat 30 times

BACKFIST STRIKES

(continued)

DESCENDING BACKFIST STRIKE TO THE FACE - URAKEN OROSHI GANMEN UCHI

1 Left fist in strike position at the face, right fist pulled back at the rib under armpit

2 Raise right fist behind the right ear, move left fist to right ribs

3 Turn the hips left, strike the right backfist down, as the left hand pulls back to the ribs

4 'Kiai' as you whip the fist at the wrist and keep the fist strong at the last second

5 Keep a good stance and posture and repeat 30 times

Rising Backfist Punch to the Solar Plexus (Pit of the Stomach) – Shitta Tsuki

1 Left hand inverted, in punching position at the solar plexus

2 Right fist pulled back to the right ribs under armpit

3 Twist wrist palm downward to prepare, turn the hips and execute the right-side punch

4 Punch the solar plexus, left fist pulls back to the ribs with a loud 'Kiai'

5 Keep a good stance and posture and repeat 30 times

HAMMERFIST STRIKES

Hammerfist strikes can be lethal at critical parts on the body. These techniques are executed with the bottom of the fist 'Tetsui' or the hammer of the fist, as the name implies.

Practise these Hammerfist strikes with the left foot forward in the 'Hour Glass' stance 'Hidari Sanchin Dachi'. Be aware of the relationship between a good stance and the power developed through the foot and respective punching arm.

1 From 'Yoi Dachi' draw your left arm in, crossing at the forearms

2 At the same time, draw the left foot in towards the right, centring your weight

3 Simultaneously move your feet into the 'Hour Glass' stance as you double block

4 Keep your posture straight

5 Bending the knees slightly

HAMMERFIST STRIKE TO THE TEMPLE - TETSUI KOMI KAMI

1 Left hand at temple height, palm up, wrist slightly bent, right hand pulled back to ribs

2 Bring the right hand up behind the ear and the left hand by the right ribs

3 Turn the hips and strike to the temple with the right hand as the left fist pulls back

4 Keep the posture straight

5 Knees slightly bent, repeat 30 times

HAMMERFIST STRIKE TO THE SPLEEN - TETSUI HIZO UCHI

1 Left hand at hip height, palm up, right hand pulled back to ribs

2 Bring the right hand up behind the ear and the left hand by the right ribs

3 Turn the hips and strike to spleen or ribs with the right hand, as the left fist pulls back

4 Keep the posture straight

5 Knees slightly bent, repeat 30 times

HAMMERFIST STRIKE TO THE GROIN TO THE SIDE - GEDAN YOKO TETSUI UCHI

1 Left hand at groin height to the side, right hand pulled back to the ribs

2 Turn the hips and raise both hands crossing at the forearms in front of the face

3 Strike down the side at the groin with the right fist, pulling the left fist back to the ribs

4 Keep the posture straight

5 Knees slightly bent, repeat 30 times

DESCENDING HAMMERFIST STRIKE TO THE FACE - TETSUI OROSHI GANMEN UCHI

1 Left fist in strike position at the face, right fist pulled back at the rib under armpit

2 Raise right fist behind the right ear, move left fist to the right ribs under armpit

3 Turn the hips, strike the right fist down to the face, the left hand pulls back to the ribs

4 Whip the fist at the wrist and keep the fist strong at the last second

5 Keep a good stance and posture and repeat 30 times

KNIFEHAND STRIKES

*Hold the hand in the knifehand position 'Shuto',
by holding the fingers straight and tightly together.
Bend the thumb down and back to keep the palm
strong. You are striking with the edge of the hand.
Remember to 'Kiai' strongly at the focus points
and when you are moving into stance.*

*Practise these punches with the right foot forward
in the 'Hour Glass' stance 'Migi Sanchin Dachi'.
Be aware of the relationship between a good
stance and the power developed through the foot
and respective punching arm.*

1 From 'Yoi Dachi' draw your right arm in, crossing at the forearms

2 At the same time draw the right foot in towards the left, centring your weight

3 Simultaneously move your feet into the 'Hour Glass' stance as you double block

4 Keep your posture straight

5 Bend at the knees

KNIFEHAND STRIKE TO THE TEMPLE - SHUTO GANMEN UCHI

1 Left hand at temple, palm up, wrist slightly bent, right hand pulled back to ribs

2 Bring the right hand up behind the ear and the left hand by the right ribs

3 Turn the hips and strike to the temple with the right hand as the left fist pulls back

4 'Kiai' strongly and keep the posture straight

5 Knees slightly bent, repeat 30 times

DESCENDING KNIFEHAND STRIKE TO THE COLLAR-BONE - SHUTO SAKOTSU UCHI

1 Left hand in strike position to collar-bone, right hand pulled back at the ribs

2 Raise right hand behind the right ear, move left hand to the right ribs under armpit

3 Turn the hips, strike the right hand down to the collar-bone, the left hand pulls back

4 Twist the wrist at the last second and 'Kiai' strongly

5 Keep a good stance and posture and repeat 30 times

KNIFEHAND STRIKE TO THE COLLAR-BONE - SHUTO SAKOTSU UCHI KOMI

1 Left hand in strike position to collar-bone, right hand pulled back at the ribs

2 Left fingertips forward, turn the hips, thrust out right spear hand to the collar-bone

3 Tilt the right hand upwards at the last second, striking knifehand to the collar-bone

4 Left hand pulls back by the ribs, 'Kiai' loudly

5 Keep good posture, stay in your stance, repeat 30 times

Knifehand Strikes

(continued)

Knifehand Strike to the Spleen - Shuto Hizo Uchi

1 Left hand at hip height, palm up, right hand pulled back to ribs

2 Bring the right hand up behind the ear and the left hand by the right ribs

3 Turn the hips, strike to spleen or ribs with the knifehand, as the left hand pulls back

4 'Kiai' strongly, keeping the posture straight

5 Knees slightly bent, repeat 30 times

KNIFEHAND STRIKE TO THE NECK - SHUTO KUBI UCHI

1 Left hand in strike position at neck height, right pulled back by the ribs

2 Bring the right hand palm to the opposite ear and left hand by the right ribs

3 Turn the hips, striking diagonally down on the neck, elbow slightly bent with loud 'Kiai'

4 Left hand pulls back by the left ribs, keeping the posture straight

5 Stay in a good 'Sanchin Dachi' with your knees slightly bent

ELBOW STRIKES

Strikes with the elbow, being generated from the body movement in the hips, are very powerful. Do not strike directly on the end of the elbow – use the elbow end of the forearm or just back from the point of the elbow.

Practise these elbow strikes with the left foot forward in the 'Hour Glass' stance 'Hidari Sanchin Dachi'. Be aware of the relationship between a good stance and the power developed through the foot and respective punching arm.

1 From 'Yoi Dachi' draw your left arm in, crossing at the forearms

2 At the same time draw the left foot in towards the right, centring your weight

3 Move the same foot left into the 'Hour Glass' stance as you double block with a 'Kiai'

4 Keep your posture straight

5 Bend the knees slightly

ELBOW STRIKE TO THE MID-SECTION - CHUDAN HIJI ATE

1 Left elbow bent at the solar plexus height, right fist back at the ribs

2 Hips turn, right fist thrusts to punch, then elbow bends just before striking solar plexus

3 Left hand retracts back to the left ribs with a strong 'Kiai'

4 Keep your posture straight

5 Stay in a strong stance, knees slightly bent, repeat 30 times

FRONT ELBOW STRIKE TO THE MID-SECTION - CHUDAN MAE HIJI ATE

1 Left elbow bent at mid-section height, right fist back at the ribs

2 Hips turn, right elbow comes around at hip height and lifts to strike the solar plexus

3 Left hand retracts back to the left ribs with a strong 'Kiai'

4 Keep your posture straight

5 Stay in a strong stance, knees slightly bent, repeat 30 times

FRONT ELBOW STRIKE TO THE CHIN - JODAN MAE HIJI ATE

1 Left elbow bent at chin height, right fist back at the ribs

2 Hips turn, right elbow comes around at chest height and lifts to strike the chin

3 Left hand retracts back to the left ribs with a strong 'Kiai'

4 Keep your posture straight

5 Stay in a strong stance, knees slightly bent, repeat 30 times

ELBOW STRIKE TO THE HEAD - JODAN HIJI ATE

1 Left elbow bent at chin height, right fist back at the ribs

2 Turn the hips, right fist thrusts to punch, then elbow bends just before striking the chin

3 Left hand retracts back to the left ribs with a strong 'Kiai'

4 Keep your posture straight

5 Stay in a strong stance, knees slightly bent, repeat 30 times

RISING ELBOW STRIKE TO THE CHIN - AGE HIJI ATE

1 Palm of the left fist at the left ear, elbow at chin level, right hand pulled back

2 Turn the hips and thrust the right elbow straight up with a loud 'Kiai'

3 The left hand retracts back beside the ribs

4 Keep your posture straight

5 Stay in a strong stance, knees slightly bent, repeat 30 times

ELBOW STRIKE TO THE REAR - USHIRO HIJI ATE

1 Looking over your right shoulder, right elbow behind, left hand on right fist

2 Thrust both hands to the front, turn the hips, and drive the left elbow behind

3 Reinforce the elbow with the right hand into the solar plexus and 'Kiai' loudly

4 Keep your posture straight

5 Stay in a strong stance, knees slightly bent, repeat 30 times

KICKS

Kicks are a strong part of your karate. Distinct from your hand techniques, kicks provide 'distance' in your self-defence. The same principles apply to your kicks as to your blocks and strikes – technique and speed. Remember to take it incrementally if you are just beginning.

Use the left foot 'Forward Leaning' stance - 'Hidari Zenkutsu Dachi' for the front stretch kicks.

1 From 'Yoi Dachi' left palm of fist to the opposite ear as the right protects the groin

2 Drive the right leg back and block down lower block 'Gedan Barai'

3 Left knee bent at a right angle, just seeing your toes over the knee

4 Both legs shoulder-width apart, right leg straight, foot 45 degrees

5 Stay deep in the stance during all kicks

FRONT STRETCH KICK - MAE KEAGE

1 Hands up, eyes straight ahead

2 Kick the left leg up to head height, keeping the knee straight

3 Foot in 'ball of foot' position, 'Chusoku'

4 Concentrate on stretching the hamstring and glutes (back of thighs and legs)

5 Repeat 20 times then do the other leg

SIDE STRETCH KICK - YOKO KEAGE

1 Hands on your belt or hips

2 Lift left leg to the side, keep the left leg straight

3 Foot stays in 'Knife edge of the foot' position 'Sokuto'.

4 Stretching the adductors (inner thighs) of the kicking leg and the hamstrings of the stationary leg

5 Alternate from left to right for momentum, concentrate on the stretch

Use the 'Closed Foot' stance - 'Heisoku Dachi' for the 'Side Stretch Kick' - 'Yoko Keage'

1 From 'Yoi Dachi'

2 Right foot moves to the left foot so they are closed

3 At the same time both palms position by the sides of the legs

Use the 'Free' stance - 'Fudo Dachi' for the following kicks.

1 From 'Yoi Dachi'

2 Both hands come up for head cover

3 Legs are relaxed

SNAP KICK TO THE GROIN - KIN GERI

1 Hands up, eyes straight ahead

2 Hips thrust forward, left knee comes up high

3 Knee extends as lower leg snaps up kicking the groin with instep 'Heisoku'

4 'Kiai' loudly and place the foot back on the floor with speed

5 Alternate legs 20 times each

FRONT SNAP KICK TO THE SOLAR PLEXUS - CHUDAN MAE GERI

1 Hands up, eyes straight ahead

2 Hips thrust forward, left knee comes up high, knee extends

3 Lower leg snaps up kicking the solar plexus with the ball of the foot 'Chusoku'

4 'Kiai' loudly and place the foot back on the floor with speed

5 Alternate legs 20 times each

KICKS

(continued)

FRONT SNAP KICK TO THE FACE - JODAN MAE GERI

1 Hands up, eyes straight ahead

2 Hips thrust forward, left knee comes up high, knee extends

3 Lower leg snaps up kicking the face with the ball of the foot 'Chusoku'

4 'Kiai' loudly and place the foot back on the floor with speed

5 Alternate legs 20 times each

KNEE TO THE FACE - HIZA GANMEN GERI

1 Hands up, eyes straight ahead, both hands reach forward grabbing the head

2 Hips thrust forward, hands bring head down as the left knee comes up high,

3 Knee hits face with loud 'Kiai'

4 Place the foot back on the floor with speed

5 Alternate legs 20 times each

SIDE KICK TO THE HEAD - JODAN YOKO GERI

1 Hands up, eyes look to the right

2 Left knee comes up high, hips turn, and the right foot pivots heel to the left

3 Hip and knee extend, foot kicks to the head and face, knife edge of the foot 'Sokuto'

4 Loud 'Kiai', place the foot back on the floor with speed

5 Alternate legs 20 times each

SIDE KICK TO THE MID-SECTION - CHUDAN YOKO GERI

1 Hands up, eyes look to the right

2 Left knee comes up high, hips turn, and the right foot pivots heel to the left

3 Hip and knee extend, foot kicks to the solar plexus, knife edge of the foot 'Sokuto'

4 Loud 'Kiai', place the foot back on the floor with speed

5 Alternate legs 20 times each

SIDE KICK TO THE KNEE JOINT - KANSETSU GERI

1 Hands up, eyes look to the right

2 Left knee comes up high, hips turn, and the right foot pivots heel to the right

3 Hip and knee extend, foot kicks the knee joint using knife edge of the foot 'Sokuto'

4 Loud 'Kiai', place the foot back on the floor with speed

5 Alternate legs 20 times each

KICKS

(continued)

BACK KICK TO THE MID-SECTION - CHUDAN USHIRO GERI

1 Look over the shoulder with peripheral vision, hands up

2 Lean upper body forward, driving left foot straight back into the solar plexus

3 'Kiai' loudly kicking with the heel 'Kakato'

4 Place the foot back on the floor with speed

5 Alternate legs 20 times each

CRESCENT KICK FROM THE INSIDE OUTWARDS – UCHI MAWASHI GERI

1 Hands up, eyes straight ahead

2 Left leg crosses to the right side of the body

3 Then comes up and arcs from the right to the left, with a 'Kiai'

4 Blocking an attack or kicking to the side of the face with 'Sokuto'

5 Place the foot back on the floor with speed, alternate legs 20 times each

CRESCENT KICK FROM THE OUTSIDE INWARDS – SOTO MAWASHI GERI

1 Hands up, eyes straight ahead

2 Left leg extends to the left side of the body

3 Then comes up and arcs from the left to the right, with a 'Kiai'

4 Blocking an attack or kicking to the side of the face with 'Sokuto'

5 Place the foot back on the floor with speed, alternate legs 20 times each

ROUND HOUSE KICK TO THE THIGH – GEDAN MAWASHI GERI

1 Hands up, eyes straight ahead

2 Left knee come up high and to the side

3 Hips turn, right foot pivots heel to the front, lower leg extends at the knee

4 Strong 'Kiai' as the shin 'Sune' kicks the thigh

5 Place the foot back on the floor with speed, alternate legs 20 times each

KICKS

(continued)

ROUND HOUSE KICK TO THE MID-SECTION - CHUDAN MAWASHI GERI

1 Hands up, eyes straight ahead

2 Left knee comes up high and to the side

3 Hips turn, right foot pivots heel to the front, lower leg extends at the knee

4 Strong 'Kiai' as the ball of the foot 'Chusoku' kicks the solar plexus or ribs

5 Place the foot back on the floor with speed, alternate legs 20 times each

ROUND HOUSE KICK TO THE HEAD - JODAN MAWASHI GERI

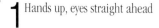

1 Hands up, eyes straight ahead

2 Left knee come up high and to the side

3 Hips turn, right foot pivots heel to the front, lower leg extends at the knee

4 Strong 'Kiai' as the instep of the foot 'Heisoku' kicks the head

5 Place the foot back on the floor with speed, alternate legs 20 times each

DEEP BREATHING - NOGARE

Deep breathing is used to help lower the heart rate and recover from intense exercise, reducing oxygen loss in the body. It is advisable to practise deep breathing any time you are in this condition. Whilst deep breathing, take the opportunity to focus on improving your training. Be aware of your goals and do not take too many breaks for 'Nogare'.

Stand in 'Ready' stance - 'Yoi Dachi' for 'Deep Breathing' - 'Nogare'

1 Upright posture

2 Shoulders relaxed

3 Arms crossed with fists at opposite shoulders

4 Feet shoulder width apart and pigeon-toed 45 degrees inward

5 Block down with both arms as your feet move 45 degrees outward

6 Fists positioned approx. two fist-lengths in front of each thigh

7 Elbows and knees slightly bent

'Deep Breathing' - 'Nogare'

1 Cross your arms, exhaling any remaining air from the lungs

2 Inhale slowly, breathing in to your abdomen

3 Lift your hands to your ribs, opening your chest

4 Then exhale and cross your arms, exhaling any remaining air from the lungs

5 Repeat 10 times slowing your breathing down as you proceed.

STRENGTH EXERCISES

Body strength exercises are a good way to condition the body. There are suitable modifications to suit the complete beginner right through to the advanced student.

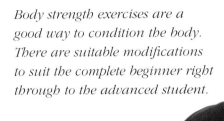

PUSH-UPS ON THE KNUCKLES

1 Fists on the floor directly below the shoulders

2 Raise your body off the floor drawing your stomach in to your spine

3 Shoulders, hips, knees and ankles should be in line with each other

4 Bend the elbows at right angles so your chest and chin are nearly to the floor

5 Elbows stay close to the ribs as you execute your push-ups

6 Aim for 20 repetitions

7 Try modifications on your knees, on your hands, or both

CRUNCHES

1 Lay on your back on the floor, knees bent, feet on the floor

2 Draw your stomach into your spine, hands behind your head

3 Inhale to prepare, exhale flexing the torso

4 Chin into the chest, looking at the knee

5 Keep your lower back on the floor, try for 20 repetitions

SQUATS

1 Hands by your sides, back straight

2 Draw the stomach into the spine

3 Inhale, lower the body, flexing the hip, knee and ankle

4 Exhale, come back up, extending the hip, knee and ankle

5 Try for 20 repetitions

FOCUS & MEDITATION EXERCISE

Stand in the 'Back' stance - 'Kokutsu Dachi' and hold a 'Knifehand Front Round Block' - 'Shuto Mae Mawashi Uke'

1 From 'Ready' stance 'Yoi Dachi' left foot comes forward

2 Bending low on the right leg

3 Both hands palm in palm, start forward and pull back to the right ribs

4 Hands turn a full circle over the head on the right side of the body

5 Left hand comes forward into knifehand, right hand comes back to ribs

6 Close your eyes or look at one point only

7 Concentrate on your breathing and focus on your training

8 Try to hold for 2 minutes and alternate legs, increasing duration each time

THE BOW-OUT
THE END OF THE CLASS

REFER TO STEPS FROM PAGES 12 AND 13 OF THE BOW-IN

1 Stand in 'Ready' stance 'Yoi Dachi'

2 Move in to 'Formal Attention' stance 'Musubi Dachi'

3 Move into a kneeling position 'Seiza'

4 Bow to the front 'Shinzen Ni Rei'

5 Close your eyes 'Mokuso'

6 Bow to the front again 'Sosai ni rei'

7 Bow again, this time to each other (if practising in a class situation) 'Sensei Ni Rei'

    1 Bow to each other, in acknowledgment and respect, as teacher and student

    2 Both fists go to the floor approx. two fist-lengths in front of the knees

    3 Bowing forward, the elbows bend as your head nearly touches the floor

    4 As you bow say 'Osu'

    5 Move straight back to kneeling position 'Seiza'

MOVING BASICS -
'Ido Geiko'

The purpose of moving basics is to take the technical basics you have been practising repetitively and use them in moving form. This will help develop timing of movement and execution of technique, balance, and practical application.

ONE STEP MOVING BASICS - KIHON IPPON

SET 1

1 Step forward in 'Forward' stance 'Zenkutsu Dachi'

2 Step back in 'Forward' stance 'Zenkutsu Dachi'

SET 2

1 Step forward in 'Forward' stance 'Zenkutsu Dachi', attacking with a mid-section punch 'Chudan Oi Tsuki' to the solar plexus

2 Step back in 'Forward' stance 'Zenkutsu Dachi', defending with a 'Mid-Section Outside Inward' block 'Chudan Soto Uke' and retaliating with an 'Upper Reverse' punch 'Jodan Gyaku Tsuki' to the face

Moving Basics

(continued)

Set 3

1 Step forward in 'Forward' stance 'Zenkutsu Dachi', attacking with a 'Mid-Section' punch 'Chudan Oi Tsuki' to the solar plexus

2 Step back in 'Forward' stance 'Zenkutsu Dachi', defending with a 'Mid-Section Inside Outward' block 'Chudan Uchi Uke', and retaliating with a 'Lower Reverse' punch 'Gedan Gyaku Tsuki' to the groin

SET 4

1 Step forward in 'Forward' stance 'Zenkutsu Dachi', attacking with an 'Upper' punch 'Jodan Oi Tsuki' to the chin

2 Step back in 'Forward' stance 'Zenkutsu Dachi', defending with an 'Upper' block 'Jodan Uke' and retaliating with a 'Mid-Section Reverse' punch 'Chudan Gyaku Tsuki' to the solar plexus

MOVING BASICS

(continued)

SET 5

1 Step forward in 'Forward' stance 'Zenkutsu Dachi', attacking with a 'Lower' punch 'Gedan Oi Tsuki' to the groin

2 Step back in 'Forward' stance 'Zenkutsu Dachi', defending with a 'Lower' block 'Gedan Barai' and retaliating with an 'Upper Reverse' punch 'Jodan Gyaku Tsuki' to the chin

SET 6

1 Step forward in 'Forward' stance 'Zenkutsu Dachi', attacking with a 'Mid-Section Front Kick' 'Chudan Mae Geri' to the solar plexus

2 Step back in 'Forward' stance 'Zenkutsu Dachi', defending with a 'Lower' block 'Gedan Barai' and retaliating with a 'Mid-Section Round House' kick 'Chudan Mawashi Geri' to the ribs or kidneys

SELF-DEFENCE

Stand-up grappling self-defence is just as important in karate as the blocks, punches, strikes and kicks. Grappling is more advanced and is best learned with a partner. The following is some basic grappling self-defence to begin with.

SET 1

1 The attacker grabs the defender's shoulders from behind

2 The defender steps forward, pulling attacker off balance

3 The defender turns head right, raises right hand, turns hips and body right, claiming attacker's right arm

4 The defender steps left leg forward, places left hand on attacker's right shoulder

5 Defender steps right leg back, pulling defender forward off balance

6 Defender turns hips and body to the right, pulls arm with right hand and pushes shoulder with left hand, takes attacker to the ground

SELF-DEFENCE

(continued)

SET 2

1 The attacker grabs the defender's shoulders from the front

2 The defender claims the attacker's left hand with their left hand

3 The defender raises right arm

4 The defender turns the hips and body left, weaves right arm over attacker's left arm and under their right arm, releases claimed arm and places it with their opposite hand in prayer-like position

5 The defender turns hips and body right, pushes attacker away and off-balance with reinforced arms

6 The defender claims right arm and pulls with right hand, pushes left forearm on attacker's right tricep, takes attacker to the ground

SELF-DEFENCE

(continued)

SET 3

1 The attacker grabs defender from behind in a bear hug

2 The defender keeps their chin down, punches forward with both hands throwing hips back

3 The defender drives back with left elbow

4 The defender claims attacker's left arm with right hand, raises left arm

5 The defender keeps their weight low, places attacker's elbow over shoulder, turns attacker's wrist to the left with both hands

6 The defender pulls down with hands, keeping body upright, puts pressure on attacker's right elbow, takes attacker to the ground

CONCLUSION

Thank you for training with SIMPLY KARATE. Remember, self-improvement involves two components;

1) *Correct instruction* – make sure you refer to this book and the DVD often to check the application of your technique;

2) *Self effort* – this means a lot of perspiration on your part, so refer to the class section on the DVD.

It is advisable to train at least two or three times a week to maintain your focus and your body's adjustment to training. However, if you are serious about karate, training daily is the key. This does not necessarily mean you have to train the whole karate class every day. Make sure that you spend time on different aspects of your karate, such as your blocks or your focus exercise.

Your posture and stance are important areas to work on. Take a look through the book and choose an area you would like to focus on. Practise the moves with good technique in your own time, then queue the DVD to the corresponding class section and train the same technique with speed, focus, good posture and stance, aiming to stay with the class.

There are so many components to your karate. Those outlined here in SIMPLY KARATE are just the basic foundation for good karate! I must emphasise that enjoying your training comes to you on the road of learning, and that the rewards are great if your training is smart and vigorous. Throughout your training, your physical fitness and flexibility will improve along with your knowledge of karate and self-defence.

I wish you all the best and hope that SIMPLY KARATE helps you either as a successful introduction to karate, or as a helpful tool to supplement your training.

Osu.

ABOUT THE AUTHOR

MARK RICHARDSON discovered martial arts in Japan at the age of six and became a student of 'Kyokushinkai Karate' on the Gold Coast, Australia at age ten. His love of the art and his competition experience sparked an interest in boxing and other martial arts, developing in him a positive attitude and interest in health and fitness.

Mark went on to study Sports Management and Marketing at Griffith University and Exercise Science at the AIF. His studies have led him to a successful career as a personal trainer at Pulse Health Studio in Broadbeach, Queensland, Australia and as a karate instructor.

Mark's extensive experience and knowledge of the martial arts has already given him the opportunity to present the kick boxercise workout DVD and book FIGHTING FIT; and the cardio and strength workout DVD and book SIMPLY BALL & BAND.

Now Mark is pleased to bring you the SIMPLY KARATE workout book and DVD set. He anticipates that it will offer you a range of physical challenges and at the same time keep your training fun. Look out for Mark in future releases of martial arts, cardio and strength training, so you can add a variety of overall health, fitness and well-being titles to your collection.